A Message from the President

The establishment at Rosemoor o… d garden is a most exciting and progressive initia… he development of Rosemoor, already warml… Country, gives a focal point to the Society's act… garden of excellence and education for visitors to enjoy at any time of the year.

The Society is greatly indebted to Lady Anne Palmer for the most generous gift, in 1988, of her house and garden at Rosemoor, together with an additional 32 acres of pasture land. This has enabled the Society to begin to plan the development of a nationally important garden in the heart of Devon, and one which should become a centre for horticulture in the region.

We are particularly fortunate that the eight-acre garden designed and developed by Lady Anne should contain such a superb range of garden plants, as well as many unusual species originating from seed collected by her in the wild. It is also a very personal garden, with a fine understanding of the use of shape, colour and contrast in its plantings, which the Society is determined to maintain.

The first phase of the New Garden, together with the new Visitors Centre and its fine facilities, opened in June 1990. As time progresses many new features will be developed, with model gardens, trials, extensive herbaceous borders and arboretum plantings, amongst others. Alongside these, for members of the Society, numerous lectures, demonstrations and garden walks are held throughout the year.

The establishment of Rosemoor as one of the first RHS centres which it is intended to develop throughout the country is, therefore, very important and I hope that many of you who visit Rosemoor and see what we are aiming to achieve will want to join the Society and support us in this exciting and challenging task. I am sure that you will thoroughly enjoy your visit and hope that you will return, not only to renew your acquaintance with the original garden, but also to witness a national garden in the making.

Robin Herbert

Robin Herbert
President
The Royal Horticultural Society

TORRINGTON
FOR DETAILS OF
LADY ANNE'S GARDEN
SEE FACING PAGE
STREAM GARDEN
UNDERPASS
(SEE BOTTOM LEFT
FACING PAGE)
N
W
E
S
B3220
LONG BORDER
SQUARE
GARDEN
SHRUB
ROSE
GARDEN
PLANT
SALES
CENTRE
CAR
PARK
SPIRAL
GARDEN
MODERN
ROSE
GARDEN
VISITORS CENTRE
RESTAURANT
RED ARROWHEADS
INDICATE ROUTE AS
DESCRIBED IN THIS
GUIDE
OVERFLOW CAR PARK
PICNIC AREA

LADY ANNE'S GARDEN

Introduction

Nestling in the wooded valley of the River Torridge, Rosemoor is a delightful garden, incorporating a diverse mixture of gardening styles, in a beautiful setting. Side by side at Rosemoor are the very personal garden created by Lady Anne Palmer, VMH, and the new garden area containing many interesting and exciting features, continually being added to in furtherance of the Society's Master Plan for the development of Rosemoor.

Rosemoor Garden was generously given to the Royal Horticultural Society by Lady Anne Palmer in 1988, together with the rest of the Rosemoor Estate, amounting in total to some 16 hectares (40 acres). The Estate had been owned by Lady Anne's family since 1923, and the house was originally used as a fishing lodge. Rosemoor is the Society's first Regional Garden, incorporating a Regional Centre. As such its principal remit is to serve RHS members (and widen membership) in the South-west, and to provide facilities for affiliated

Rosemoor House, from across the Pond in Lady Anne's Garden

organisations.

The garden lies one mile south of the town of Great Torrington, on the west-facing slopes of the Torridge valley, at around 30 metres (98 feet) above sea level. It is bisected by the B3220 road to Exeter, and enclosed on all sides by woodland. The soil is a moderately acid silty clay loam, with a pH of around 5.5. Rainfall averages 1010 mm (40 inches) per year, and while the climate might overall be described as fairly mild, the valley bottom site is something of a frost pocket, and sharp frosts with minima of -9 C or below may occur in winter. Late spring frosts which can damage flowers and young growths are also a feature of the area.

Development of the original garden in the north-east corner of the estate (around Rosemoor House) began in 1959, after Lady Anne Palmer met the noted plantsman Collingwood Ingram in Spain. There were already a few exotic trees growing there, for example a fine Turkey oak *(Quercus cerris)* in the Main Lawn, and two tulip trees *(Liriodendron tulipifera)* near the house. But virtually the whole garden as it exists now has been created in the last thirty years.

Thus the garden at Rosemoor breaks down into two distinct areas: the original garden, now called Lady Anne's Garden, and the New Garden Area. The latter is effectively all of the Estate outside of Lady Anne's original garden. The initial developments in the New Garden are concentrated around the new Visitors Centre, and along the paths which lead to Lady Anne's Garden, all to the west of the B3220. The two halves of the garden, east and west, are joined by an underpass, which emerges into Lady Anne's Garden at the southern end of the Arboretum.

This guide will take the visitor on a circular tour, beginning at the garden entrance in the Visitors Centre, taking in the New Garden Area, thence to Lady Anne's Garden, and finally ending back at the Visitors Centre.

A Guide to Rosemoor

On entering Rosemoor, the attractiveness of its setting is immediately obvious, with the steep wooded valley slopes rising to the west beyond the River Torridge. Around the entrance and car park, and in the Parkland to the south, are planted groups of mainly large-growing forest trees in a range of genera including *Tilia* (lime), *Fraxinus* (ash), *Fagus* and *Nothofagus* (beech and southern beech), and *Quercus* (oak). On either side of the entrance two groups of the weeping silver lime *(Tilia petiolaris)*, will rapidly form an imposing feature.

The plantings are designed to provide an attractive open parkland, which also accommodates the overflow car park and picnic area.

This aerial photograph well shows the layout of the Visitors Centre and Plant Centre. The two rose gardens are to the right

The Visitors Centre

Completed in spring 1990, the new Visitors Centre at Rosemoor is a most distinguished building, with numerous facilities for visitors. The Restaurant, housed in the south wing, is open during the season at the same hours as the Garden, and serves a range of delicious light meals and snacks. To the right of the entrance foyer, the Shop carries a fine selection of horticultural books, as well as many other attractive and desirable gifts and souvenirs. Immediately outside the Shop is the Plant Sales Centre. Here you will find a wide range of interesting and unusual plants, a good proportion of which have been raised at Rosemoor, reflecting the mix of plants growing in the garden.

The Visitors Centre has been built on a platform overlooking the Formal Garden in the Square Field to the west. The Courtyard immediately outside is bounded by the Restaurant and Plant Sales Centre to the left and right respectively. Future plans for this area include a further wing on the north side of the Courtyard, identical to the Restaurant, which will house a lecture theatre. To the south of the Restaurant a terrace area, with raised beds for alpine plants, also serves as an overflow for the restaurant during busy periods.

The Courtyard and Terrace

In the Courtyard four specimens of *Acer palmatum* 'Osakazuki' have been planted in the L-shaped beds. These will slowly grow into large spreading bushes, with attractive foliage and fine autumn colour. Initial plantings in the Courtyard include many tender perennials for summer display, with the same theme predominating in the beds alongside the ramps leading down to the Formal Garden.

The east face of the Visitors Centre

The construction of the platform upon which the Visitors Centre sits provides a generous stretch of west-facing wall immediately below the Terrace. The plantings here are designed to reflect the ethos of Rosemoor as created by Lady Anne Palmer, with a mixture of plants including many which are rare and unusual, particularly from the Southern Hemisphere, grown here to take advantage of the shelter given by the wall.

The plantings include many climbers and shrubs. A good representation of shrubby daisy family plants includes several species of *Olearia* from Australasia, and the striking *Pachystegia insignis* from New Zealand, closely related to olearias, but with broad leathery rhododendron-like leaves. Other genera from south of the Equator include *Myrtus* and *Lophomyrtus, Drimys, Acca (Feijoa), Pittosporum*, and *Eucryphia*, all good evergreen subjects, which thrive in the mild and moist climate of the south-west.

The Courtyard to the west of the Visitors Centre

The Formal Garden

Occupying the entire 3 hectares (7.5 acres) of the Square Field, the Formal Garden is the most intensively cultivated area at Rosemoor. A variety of distinctive gardens and other features are being developed, designed around the strong formal axes running east-west from the Visitors Centre, and north-south across the width of the Square Field. These gardens and borders contain a blend of plantings for display and demonstration, designed both to please the eye, and to educate the visitor.

The Visitors Centre terrace is raised 2.4 metres (8 feet) above the Formal Garden, and from the top of the steps leading down affords a fine view along the east-west axis to the wooded slopes beyond. From this point the four Formal Square Gardens at the heart of the Square Field can be seen, enclosed within a yew hedge *(Taxus baccata)*. Along the east-west and north-south axes, the hedge will eventually reach some 2.4 metres (8 feet) high, enclosing the gardens from view, and providing a backdrop for the mixed double border which will run from south to north along the entire 180 metre (200 yard) width of the field.

The Modern Rose Garden, seen from the Terrace of the Visitors Centre

The Rose Gardens

The first two Formal Squares immediately below the Terrace are dedicated to roses, and were planted in spring 1990. On the left, the Modern Rose Garden contains 1500 plants, in 60 cultivars. Here hybrid tea and floribunda roses predominate (recently reclassified as large- and cluster-flowered respectively), with a mixture of climbing varieties in these groups to clothe the obelisk-shaped pillars. The cultivars have been carefully chosen for resistance to disease, which can be a particular problem in the clean air and rather soft and damp growing conditions which prevail in the West Country. They are also fine and vigorous examples in the range of colours and sizes represented, with scent also being an important criterion for inclusion.

To the right of the east-west axis, the flowing lines of the Shrub Rose Garden contrast strongly with the more angular design of its neighbour. In the larger of the two ovals is a catenary, effectively a number of pillars to support climbers and ramblers, with a rope joining them, along which the stronger-growing cultivars are trained. The Shrub Rose Garden contains a diverse collection, with 130 cultivars amongst the nearly 500 roses. In the two ovals older groups such as gallica, alba and centifolia roses predominate, whilst in the outer beds many more modern cultivars may be found. The groups represented take the story of shrub roses from hundreds of years ago to the present day, with modern hybrids such as English Roses demonstrating up-to-the-minute developments in breeding in this group. To complement this collection, a wide range of other interesting shrub and species roses may be seen in Lady Anne's Garden.

Amongst the shrub roses are a number of companion plantings to enhance the overall effect, and prolong the season of display. Silver foliage and pastel-coloured flowers are especially valuable for this purpose, as also are plants such as garden pinks (*Dianthus* cultivars), with a colour range that complements the roses well, and whose foliage effect is also of value. The rich scents of the majority of the shrub roses, alongside those of the pinks, make the Shrub Rose Garden a delight for nose and eye from early to mid-summer.

Colour Theme Gardens

The lower two formal squares are given over to colour theme gardens. Their internal designs, as those of the rose gardens, contrast strongly. Below the Modern Rose Garden, the Spiral Garden, as its name suggests, is laid out with a path which makes its way around the area, spiralling in towards the centre. This shape is echoed by a hedge within the borders, the spiral ending where a paved area contains a semi-circular seat at the heart of the garden. Here the overall effect is one of soft flower colours and tones, complemented by silver and variegated foliage. Shrubs provide the backbone of the borders, whose colours flow from pale yellow and green through pale blue to mauve and violet, then pink, peach and apricot to buff, gradually fading in the centre to predominantly white and grey.

Below the Shrub Rose Garden the Square Garden is a complete contrast in

A section of the Long Border, with the catenary in the Shrub Rose Garden behind

design and colour. Here hot colours predominate, in an area more rigidly divided than the Spiral Garden, with contrasting foliage colours used in the hedging also. The central area of the garden, designed as a small, intimate enclosure, has the hottest colours of rust, yellow, orange and red, with yellow used as the unifying colour throughout the entire area.

The Long Border

Between the upper and lower Formal Squares, a double herbaceous border is destined to run the full width of the Square Field. The borders have been designed to provide colour from late spring until early autumn, and the initial sections, planted in spring 1990, have established well. The border is divided into discreet sections within low yew 'walls', each of which may be seen as a border in itself, but which may also be seen as a part of the greater border from a distance. The individual borders have a strong backbone of shrub planting, with long drifts of herbaceous plants to the rear, becoming more intimate in scale towards the front.

The colour scheme of the first section uses flowers of mainly pink, mauve-blue, white and soft yellow, with silver, blue and purple foliage. Amongst the larger-growing perennials, several *Thalictrum* cultivars make effective back-border subjects, with delicate glaucous foliage, and white or yellow flowers. Another back border plant, the plume poppy, *Macleaya microcarpa* 'Kelway's Coral Plume', provides a much heavier effect with its handsome grey-green lobed leaves, overtopped by delicate airy sprays of pink. Amongst other tall-growing perennials are numerous cultivars of *Delphinium, Campanula*, and monkshoods *(Aconitum).*

In the centre and front of the borders a range of hardy geraniums, *Hemerocallis* (daylilies), and *Anemone* cultivars provide a succession of flowers from spring through to early autumn. Amongst and between the perennials,

***Rosa* 'Graham Thomas', a recently bred cultivar in the Shrub Rose Garden**

summer-flowering bulbous subjects such as lilies, alliums and galtonias contribute to the overall display, as where *Allium giganteum*, with its rounded pink flower heads rises amongst the soft yellow spikes of *Verbascum* 'Gainsborough'.

As the border is developed in both directions along the central axis, so further themes and variations in colour will be introduced, until it reaches its full length of 180 metres (nearly 200 yards). Taking the fact that the plantings are on both sides of the path, in due course almost a quarter of a mile of mixed border will occupy the entire width of the Formal Garden.

Eventually, the entire Square Field will be taken up with gardens. The next phase of development will see the first Demonstration Gardens built, in the north-east corner. Here various themes with a common thread will be explored, in this instance a number of gardens characterised by the lack of large areas of grass, and the use of considerable amounts of hard surfacing with raised beds and borders. Examples of these are a Jardin Potager (a formal French-style herb and vegetable garden), a Cottage Garden, a garden for the disabled, and a Scented Garden.

To the south of the Formal Squares gardens will be developed which take into account the influence of the large trees nearby, particularly their shade. A Shade Garden will demonstrate how to overcome the problems caused by shade from trees or buildings, a Patio Garden will show a range of surfacings, suitable for areas close to the house, and the use of plants in a more architectural sense.

Specialist borders and gardens will also be created, for example a Woodland Garden in the heavily shaded south-west corner. A Foliage Garden is planned, as also are a range of borders concentrating upon plants in each of the seasons. In a Plantsman's Garden local plants will be featured, (those introduced by West Country gardeners), and around three sides of the field wide shrub plantings will include local specialities, such as Rosemoor's two collections held under the auspices of the National Council for the Conservation of Plants and Gardens, in *Ilex* (holly) and *Cornus* (dogwoods).

Towards Lady Anne's Garden

To reach Lady Anne's Garden, take the track along the centre of the Square Field through the gap in the hedge. As the track rounds the large oak to the left, a young plant of the Lucombe Oak, *Quercus* x *hispanica* 'Lucombeana' may be seen, planted to mark the opening of the new garden in June 1990. The track then leads down to a small bridge over a spring-fed stream. The path leading to the underpass and Lady Anne's Garden bears to the right.

To the west of the small bridge the stream makes its way through a small valley towards the woodland below. This area has been turned into a water and bog garden by damming the stream to create a number of ponds, with bold sweeps of marginal planting in the wet areas around.

Due north, the town of Torrington lies on a ridge above the steeply sloping common land which surrounds it on three sides. The buildings at the edge of the field were at one time part of the dairy at Rosemoor, and include a large barn known locally as a Shippen. This building is now used for machinery and equipment storage. Nearby a number of tunnel houses and beds comprise the nursery, which grows much of the material sold in the Plant Sales Centre, as well as plants for the garden proper.

In due course the area of the Shippen Field will also house the Model Fruit and Vegetable Garden which will demonstrate techniques of growing and varieties appropriate for local conditions.

The Underpass joining the two halves of Rosemoor was built in 1989. The slopes created by the need to cut into the ground to build the underpass and paths have been treated in two ways. In the long term it is intended that the slopes will be terraced with large pieces of local stone. Short term cover and protection from erosion has been provided by turfing. The steepness of the slope made this operation quite tricky, with the turf and topsoil liable to slide down the slope in wet weather. To overcome this problem turf blocks 10-15 cm (4-6 inches) thick were used, thereby laying the turf and the topsoil it required in one operation. Timber supports run across the slopes every 120 cm (4 feet), to help to retain the weight of turf and soil above. The stream which runs alongside the path is being developed to create further areas for marginal planting.

Beyond the underpass, immediately as one enters Lady Anne's Garden, a waterfall and associated rockwork demonstrate how the entire area will be treated in due course. Much of this area lends itself to growing woodland plants, particularly ferns, of which a selection including several native species may be seen in the waterfall area.

Lady Anne's Garden

The Underpass track emerges into Lady Anne's Garden at the south end of the Arboretum. This part of the garden is very wet, and a number of alders (*Alnus* species), which are very tolerant of damp conditions, have been planted on the left hand side of the path. Particularly striking is *Alnus rubra*, an American species with catkins 10-15 cm (4-6 inches) long in the spring, followed by bold foliage. At the end of the path, just before it emerges into the garden proper, is a planting of several different species and cultivars of dogwood, regularly stooled for their winter stem colour.

The Underpass track joins the Main Drive which effectively bisects this part of Lady Anne's Garden. Below is a vista from Rosemoor House to the pond, with beds and borders on either side containing a diverse mixture of trees, shrubs, herbaceous plants and bulbs. Below this is an area of woodland garden around the track known as Lock's Trail, parallel to the road. This track emerges behind Rosemoor House.

East of the Main Drive, and south of the house, an area of divided gardens has been developed, in many instances utilising or incorporating existing features to provide opportunities to accommodate a wide range of plants within a

Strong foliage contrasts form an important element of the plantings in Lady Anne's Garden

comparitively small space. The Kitchen Garden, Stone Garden, Tennis Court, Croquet Lawn and Woodland Garden all fall within this part of the garden. Further plantings of note are to be found around Rosemoor House itself.

Lady Anne's Garden houses a rich and varied collection of plants, many rare and unusual, with the accent particularly on trees and shrubs. A large proportion of them have been collected from the wild, many by Lady Anne Palmer herself. The botanical value of the collection is greatly enhanced by the large number of plants of known provenance grown here.

The Pond and Lawn

This description of the garden begins at the Pond, which forms the southern boundary of the Main Lawn. To the north-west of the Pond two splendid bog garden plants appreciate the plentiful moisture by the water's edge. *Gunnera manicata* dominates the area, with its 1.8 metre (6 feet) wide leaves, reminiscent of a giant rhubarb. Immediately by its side the Asiatic species of Bog Arum, *Lysichitum camtschatcense*, in any other circumstances a bold leafed perennial with 1.2m (4 feet) leaves, is positively dwarfed by its larger neighbour. The *Lysichitum* bears handsome 30 cm (1foot) high white spathes in the early spring.

Around the southern edge of the Pond more moisture-loving plants are grown, including primulas, astilbes, irises and *Peltiphyllum peltatum*, whose large round leaves follow attractive heads of pink-white flowers in spring, and colour well in autumn. Another handsome herbaceous perennial, *Filipendula palmata* 'Rosea', bears heads of pink flowers above its attractively-cut foliage in summer. Alongside this grows the curiously twisted hazel, *Corylus avellana* 'Contorta'. Growing right by the water's edge *Taxodium distichum*, the North American swamp cypress, has delicate ferny sprays of deciduous foliage which colour well in autumn.

Immediately beyond the pond is a small heather garden, with a range of heathers and dwarf conifers. Largest of the heathers is *Erica arborea* 'Gold Tips', with white flowers in early spring, and new growth distinctively tipped yellow, as its name suggests.

The Lawn Beds

Flanked on either side by planting, the Main Lawn runs from the Pond to Rosemoor House. Immediately to the left of the Pond a large island bed of herbaceous perennials contains a range of flowering and foliage subjects, planted for year-round display. This commences during winter with *Primula vulgaris* 'Sibthorpii', followed by several lungworts (*Pulmonaria* species), the most colourful of which is the intense blue *P. angustifolia* 'Azurea'. Nearby, the ferny blue-grey foliage of *Dicentra* 'Langtrees' appears in early spring, soon followed by its attractive pale mauve-pink flowers.

The island bed of herbaceous plants immediately north of the Pond

Amongst the largest-growing of perennials is the grass *Miscanthus sinensis* 'Silver Feather', whose white plumes of flower are produced during the autumn on stems which can reach 1.8 metres (6 feet). In contrast to the upright grass the bold purple leaves of *Ligularia dentata* 'Desdemona' make mounds of around 1.2 metres (4 feet). The heavy moist soil in this bed provides good conditions also for perennials which appreciate damp conditions, such as *Trollius, Astilbe, Iris pseudacorus* 'Variegatus', and several hostas. A number of *Iris sibirica* cultivars also do well in these conditions, as does the exceptionally dark purple-black *I. chrysographes* 'Black Knight'. An interesting and handsome evergreen fern, *Blechnum chilense*, grows around the specimen of *Betula papyrifera* in the centre of the bed.

Continuing along the Main Lawn, the beds to the right are each planted to follow a colour theme, the first with yellow, orange and bronze flowers and purple foliage, and the second white and silver. Amongst the trees and shrubs in this area *Thujopsis dolobrata* 'Variegata' has rather coarse cypress-like foliage, with scattered patches of creamy-white. In the next bed are several fine shrub roses, with the white *Rosa* 'Boule de Neige' covered with flowers in mid-June. Nearby is an unusual conifer, the Japanese umbrella pine, *Sciadopytis verticillata* . An interesting range of euphorbias also grows here, from the shrubby *Euphorbia characias* subsp. *wulfenii,* with glaucous foliage reaching 1.2m (4 feet), to herbaceous species such as the native *E. palustris,* with bold heads of yellow bracts, followed by fine orange autumn colour.

Autumn colour enhances the borders immediately south of Rosemoor House

Nearby a large plant of the very spiny *Colletia armata* 'Rosea' from Chile bears its small fragrant pink-white flowers in late summer and early autumn. Immediately alongside, a fine red cultivar of the quince, *Chaenomeles* x *superba*, flowers in late winter and spring. Around the *Colletia* grow a number of the blue-flowered *Agapanthus* Headbourne Hybrids, and the orange-yellow *Crocosmia* 'Lady Hamilton', for display towards the end of the summer. On the lawn side of the bed can be seen *Zenobia pulverulenta*, a glaucous ericaceous shrub, with white scented flowers in early summer. Nearby *Anaphalis margaritacea* provides silver-leaved ground cover and white everlasting flowerheads late in the season.

At the end of the Main Lawn a bright year-round effect is achieved by a golden cultivar of *Thuja plicata*, and several golden variegated phormiums. Nearby a rare conifer from New Zealand, *Podocarpus acutifolius*, has yellow-green foliage which in winter turns an attractive bronzy-gold. The road then leads on towards the Old Car Park area, and the back of Rosemoor House.

The Old Car Park

The borders along the north-west face of the house are home to a number of plants of special value during the winter. The most imposing of these is *Garrya elliptica*, with its grey catkins this is an attractive subject at a dull time of year. To the right *Viburnum tinus* 'Eve Price' has pink-white flowers in clusters. For winter scent few plants are better than *Sarcococca hookeriana*, growing by the side of the steps. Its insignificant white flowers can be smelt from a considerable distance on mild days.

The Stable Yard contains a number of interesting tender plants. *Pittosporum tenuifolium* to the left is a support for the yellow-flowered climbing daisy, *Senecio scandens.* On the wall the evergreen *Hydrangea integerrima* clings with adventitious roots. Beneath it both the handsome variegated *Cleyera fortunei* 'Variegata', from Japan, and *Illicium floridanum* from the southern USA are of note. In mid-to late winter *Ribes laurifolium*, an unusual evergreen relative of the blackcurrant from western China, bears spikes of pale yellow-green flowers on lax branches which are trained up the wall. The pots and troughs in the Stable Yard are worthy of attention, as they contain a number of interesting plants, grown here in order to take advantage of the shelter.

West of the old Car Park area is a selection of deciduous azaleas, principally of the group known as Knap Hill Hybrids. These plants make a fine display in May, with flowers in a wide range of colours. The path through this area, known as Lock's Trail, has been recently planted with a selection of interesting trees and shrubs. A mature *Magnolia* x *soulangeana* can be seen immediately to the right, beyond which is a collection of New Zealand plants, including several species of southern beech, *Nothofagus.*

Heading south into the main garden is a woodland area rich with rhododendrons and camellias. Pacific Coast hybrid irises, a large group derived from species from the western seaboard of the USA and Canada, form an underplanting with evergreen leaves which make excellent ground-cover.

On the right side of the path is a plant of *Rhododendron argyrophyllum*

A view of Lock's Trail with *Cornus* 'Eddie's White Wonder'

var. *nankingense*, from China. The undersides of the large deep green leaves have a silvery white coating, known as indumentum, beneath. Pink bell-shaped flowers over 5 cm (2 inches) across are borne in large trusses in spring. Large-leafed rhododendrons make imposing foliage plants, and a number have been planted around the garden in recent years. In complete contrast, nearby grows *Rhododendron williamsianum*, with shiny mid-green heart-shaped leaves, and bell-shaped flowers varying in colour from shell-pink to white.

A plant of special note in this area is the rare *Ehretia dicksonii*, a tender small tree with bold leaves. On the left hand side of the path are a number of fine flowering trees. The dogwood, *Cornus* 'Eddie's White Wonder', is a hybrid between two American species, with large white flowers in the spring. The white 'petals' are actually bracts, but serve the same purpose of attracting pollinators. Many dogwoods also give a fine display of autumn colour.

In addition to dogwoods Rosemoor has a good collection of magnolias, of which undoubtedly the finest is the Himalayan species *Magnolia campbellii*. The specimen here still has some way to go before it will achieve its final height. The large pink flowers appear in early spring.

Amongst the herbaceous plants two species of the wood lily *(Trillium)* are of interest. Both come from North America. *T. grandiflorum*, the wake robin, has white flowers in spring, and is a strong-growing plant for the woodland garden. *T. sessile* has purple flowers carried just above the mottled leaves. Several species of *Lindera* also grow in this area. These trees and shrubs are related to the culinary sweet bay *(Laurus nobilis)*, and some have rich autumn colour. A number of hybrid rhododendrons are to be found along the path leading towards the lawn. Nearby grows the golden-leafed form of the topal holly, *Ilex* x *attenuata* 'Sunny Foster'. Throughout this area the dwarf creeping dogwood *Cornus canadensis* may be seen. The stems create good ground cover bearing attractive white flowers during the summer. On the left the graceful lily relative, *Smilacina racemosa*, grows with a number of species and cultivars of *Hosta*, another lily relative, giving effective ground cover.

Bearing left on the grass path towards the main lawn, *Populus wilsonii* is of note, with 20 cm long (8 inches) bright green leaves. The borders on either side of the grass contain numerous rhododendrons, mainly small-growing species. On the left, plants of the dwarf, scaly, glaucous-leafed alpine species *Rhododendron impeditum* and *R. scintillans* from west China are a strong contrast to the tall-growing species which form a background to the right-hand border.

The Main Lawn

At the end of the grass path, as it emerges into the main lawn area which sweeps from the pond to the house, two plants of *Phormium tenax*, the New Zealand flax, stand on either side. Immediately ahead of the phormiums is a fine specimen of *Betula ermanii*, with striking pink-white bark. To the right the woodland theme continues with the glossy-leaved evergreen Californian bayberry, *Myrica californica*, a hardy shrub rarely seen in gardens. This is growing beneath a tree of *Magnolia* 'Maryland' (an evergreen hybrid between *M. grandiflora* and *M. virginiana)* which grows beneath a large black birch *(Betula nigra)*. A specimen of the purple Dawyck beech nearby makes a splash of colour amongst the greens of rhododendrons and *Drimys winteri* var. *latifolia*. To the rear of the bed, large bushes of *Rhododendron praevernum* bear bell-shaped pink-flushed white flowers in late winter and early spring. Low growing rhododendrons flank the path as it leads round to *Betula ermanii* again.

The value of foliage for colour in the garden can be seen from *Cornus controversa* 'Variegata' (right), and the glaucous *Rhododendron lepidostylum* in the centre

Continuing to the left towards the house, an effective ground cover in shade is provided by *Saxifraga stolonifera*, (mother of thousands), which is hardier than one might expect of a species grown principally as a house plant. Nearby grows a selected form of the

Asiatic blue poppy, *Meconopsis grandis* 'Prain's Variety'. One of the most striking trees in the garden is *Cornus controversa* 'Variegata', with horizontal tiered branching and attractive white variegated leaves. Several *Stuartia* species are planted in this area; with white or cream flowers in early summer, rich autumn colour, and attractive flaking bark, they have something to offer throughout the year.

Beyond the path leading up from Lock's Trail the North American oak-leafed *Hydrangea*, *H. quercifolia*, is a fine subject for bold foliage and autumn colour. Alongside it the evergreen *Trochodendron aralioides* is a rare evergreen shrub, of handsome habit with green flowers. A dogwood of note is the hybrid *Cornus* 'Norman Hadden' (*C. kousa* x *C. nuttallii*), grown from a plant propagated from the original specimen. Continuing towards the end of the bed amongst a number of interesting shrubs are the Tasmanian *Eucryphia milliganii*, with a profusion of small white flowers in summer, and *Parrotia persica* 'Pendula', the latter striking in its autumn colour. Flanking the entrance to the garden from the old Car Park is a variegated holly, *Ilex aquifolium* 'Handsworth New Silver' alongside which the winter-flowering *Mahonia japonica* shelters at its base a group of spring-flowering *Cyclamen repandum.*

The House and Kitchen Garden

The beds along the front and side of the house contain many tender subjects, enjoying the south-westerly aspect. The balcony provides support for the climbing rose 'Handel' with large creamy white flowers, pink-flushed as they age, and the yellow-flowered *Lonicera* x *tellmanniana*. A fine scented shrub in the border is *Viburnum carlesii* 'Diana', whose flowers open red and fade to white. Further along the border *Pachystegia insignis*, from New Zealand bears large white daisy flower-heads over its rhododendron-like leaves in summer. Aromatic shrubs and herbs, including *Cistus*, rosemary, thyme and lavender, grow in the beds and amongst the slabs on the front terrace.

On the house itself and to the left of the door grows *Rosa banksiae* 'Lutea', with a large *Wisteria sinensis* to the right, above the winter-flowering *Viburnum farreri.* The old conservatory area has several interesting climbers: *Robinia hispida*, with pink flowers, *Wisteria venusta* 'Violacea', and the pink *Clematis* 'Duchess of Albany'. Amongst the herbaceous plants the yellow iris-like *Moraea spathulata* is a rarity, and the orchid-shaped yellow blooms of *Roscoea cautleoides* beneath the *Robinia* add a note of the exotic. Several troughs in this area contain a number of interesting dwarf and alpine plants.

The path to the left leads to a fine specimen of *Prunus serrula*, whose rich mahogany-hued bark is a particularly striking feature. Directly across the path a gravel area contains the columnar *Juniperus drupacea,* with purple and

***Rosa* 'Complicata' blooming in early summer in the Kitchen Garden**

green-leafed phormiums providing an effective foliage contrast.

In the bed alongside the *Juniperus drupacea* several *Celmisia* species grow amongst dwarf rhododendrons and camellias. On the left hand side of the path a mixed planting contains another *Roscoea* species, *R. purpurea*, whose purple flowers are a striking sight in early summer. The elegant *Dierama pulcherrimum* bears long wands of hanging flowers from mid-summer onwards, ranging in colour from white through to deep purple. A number of small trees here are of interest. *Pinus mugo*, from central Europe, has slowly reached 4 metres (13 feet) high, and plays host to *Clematis chrysocoma* var. *sericea*. Further along, a sycamore cultivar, *Acer pseudoplatanus* 'Brilliantissimum' provides a colourful foliage effect, pink in spring, aging slowly through cream to yellow-green. Beneath it grows the yellow dog's tooth violet, *Erythronium* 'Pagoda'. Alongside is the fine evergreen *Lithocarpus edulis*, an oak relative, with handsome leaves up to 15 cm (6 inches) long. One of a number of interesting *Berberis* planted in this area is the evergreen *B. ilicifolia*, with glowing orange flowers in early spring.

The bark effect of *Prunus serrula* is echoed in the bed across the path by the Chinese paperbark maple, *Acer griseum*. A number of winter-flowering subjects have been planted here, with herbaceous plants and shrubs along the path to prolong the season of display, particularly by coloured or bold foliage. Notable plants in this bed include *Cornus controversa* with its tiered habit, reaching nearly 6 metres (20 feet), and *Magnolia kobus*, from Japan, planted in 1966. Beneath it and along the edge of the bed is a selection of viburnums and *Philadelphus*. This theme continues in the bed immediately opposite, the centre of which is taken up by a specimen of *Quercus petraea* 'Salicifolia', a narrow-leaved cultivar of the native sessile oak.

Beyond the *Prunus serrula* is the area known as the Old Kitchen Garden. This part of the garden contains a number of raised beds, built with stone or railway sleepers. The soil in these beds is better drained than that in the surrounding areas, suiting plants which appreciate dryer conditions. In the stone built scree bed are several New Zealand plants, including the unusual *Corokia cotoneaster* and the natural hybrid *C.* x *virgata. Hebe cupressoides* 'Boughton Dome' is another New Zealander, strongly reminiscent of a dwarf cypress as its name suggests.

The Wall Bed

In the bed across the path the Chilean shrub *Sophora macrocarpa* bears its yellow pea flowers in early spring. Several interesting ericaceous plants grow here, including the bigeneric hybrid x*Gaulnettya* 'Wisley Pearl'. The wall opposite, facing due south-west, is home to a number of tender and unusual plants. Australian callistemons, with their bottle-brush like flowers, flank it on either side, and the New Zealand shrubs *Olearia moschata* and *Cassinia leptophylla* are strongly contrasting examples of woody members of the daisy family. Nearby *Buddleia colvilei* has large deep rose-pink flowers in June.

Some interesting tender plants are also to be found along the west facing wall to the south. *Sophora microphylla* 'Dragon's Gold', is a New Zealand representative of the genus. Herbaceous peonies in front provide colour in early summer. Further to the right, *Cestrum elegans* is a striking shrub, with bright red flowers, belying the fact that it is a member of the potato family. Autumn-flowering bulbs are a prominent feature along the length of this bed, in particular pink nerines, which flower into October, and the yellow late-summer flowering *Sternbergia sicula.*

At the corner of the wall bed *Olearia* 'Waikariensis', planted in 1975, is an attractive silver-foliage shrub. Behind it *Itea ilicifolia*, with its green-white hanging racemes of flowers produced in late summer, has been trained against the wall. Two scree beds in front of the wall have been planted with a number of interesting dwarf and alpine plants. In the first *Dryas octopetala*, the mountain avens from Europe, has white flowers in spring. From the other side of the world *Helichrysum milfordiae*, a New Zealander, has furry silvery rosettes. In the second scree bed a number of other New Zealand plants are quite at home, including the spiny *Aciphylla subflabellata*, and the world's smallest conifer, *Dacrydium laxifolium* with curious bronzy grey foliage. *Trochocarpa thymifolia* from Tasmania is a rare dwarf shrub, one of a number of Tasmanian plants which grow well at Rosemoor.

Along the wall behind, a selection of climbing or wall shrubs grow, including the summer-flowering pineapple scented *Cytisus battandieri*, and *Trachelospermum jasminoides*, the latter an attractive evergreen climber with scented white flowers. Early flowers are obtained from *Clematis cirrhosa* var. *balearica*, in January in a mild season. Several species of *Phlomis*, with leaves in shades of grey and green grow in the bed below. An imposing plant of the bull bay, *Magnolia grandiflora*, fills the top corner.

***Cortaderia argentea* 'Sunningdale Silver', framed by autumn colour from *Liriodendron tulipifera* and a flowering cherry**

Towards the Stone Garden

A hedge of the American *Rosa foliolosa* divides the scree beds from the grassed area beyond, with further plantings of shrub roses, including very large plants of ramblers such as *Rosa* 'Bobbie James' and 'Paul's Himalayan Musk' in the flowering cherry trees to the west. A large plant of the pampas grass, *Cortaderia argentea* 'Sunningdale Silver', bears its 2.5 metre (8 feet) high plumes in autumn. There are several large shrub roses in the area, including *Rosa* 'Fantin-Latour'. Of special note is the handsome evergreen *Viburnum cylindricum* from China, whose leaves grow up to 20 cm (8 inches) long. *Betula medwediewii* nearby has a strongly ascendent branch habit. At the end of the bed are a number of hydrangeas, including *Hydrangea aspera* from West China, a fine summer flowering species. Backing the shrub bed is a mixed beech and holly hedge, with several flowering cherries on its west side, containing the rambling roses referred to above. The large tulip trees *(Liriodendron tulipifera)* which dominate this area were planted in 1932. To the right the coral bark maple, *Acer palmatum* 'Senkaki', has attractive pink-red stems in the winter, and beneath grows *Berberis hypokerina*, with handsome large holly-like evergreen leaves. Cyclamen, snowdrops, crocuses, and *Narcissus* species give a long season of display beneath the tulip trees.

Proceeding along the path towards the Stone Garden, to the right numerous species and cultivars of hellebore provide excellent late winter colour, ranging from pure white and green through rose to deep purple. Lenten roses, *Helleborus orientalis* forms, provide the main display here, with the deep purple *H. atrorubens* amongst the earliest to flower. The form of *H. orientalis* sometimes known as *H. guttatus* has attractive white flowers with deep purple spots within. This planting also includes the native green-flowered *H. foetidus*, and the imposing *H. argutifolius*.

On the left *Erica carnea* 'Springwood White' grows with a number of azaleas and rhododendrons. Nearby *Prunus* 'Kursar', a hybrid raised by Collingwood Ingram, bears a multitude of small pink flowers in early spring. At the point where the path divides left and right *Chamaecyparis pisifera* 'Filifera Aurea' has thread-like yellow stems, colourful throughout the year. Another strong foliage accent in this area comes from *Cotinus coggygria* 'Royal Purple', near to which is a plant of the Chilean lantern bush, *Crinodendron hookerianum,* with its distinctive hanging red flowers in early summer. The yew hedge on the left has at its base one of the finest herbaceous plants for dry shade, *Tellima grandiflora*, giving weed-proof ground cover from its evergreen foliage.

Facing page

Late winter colour on the path towards the Stone Garden, with *Prunus* 'Kursar' on the right, and the deep pink shoots of *Acer palmatum* 'Senkaki' to the rear

Stone and Woodland Gardens

The next major feature is the area known as the Stone Garden and Temple.

To the east of the Stone Garden numerous camellias brighten the early spring season. One of the most valuable of these is the hybrid *Camellia* x *williamsii* 'St Ewe', with single pink flowers borne over a long season. *Cyclamen* species thrive in the shady conditions, and some fine variants of *C. hederaefolium* show how these plants can be as valuable for their attractively marbled leaves during the winter as for their flowers, produced in autumn.

Immediately due east a gate leads to a track, from which a small flight of steps leads into the Woodland Garden, created on the steep west-facing slope. This area is planted principally with ericaceous plants, and is most attractive in springtime when azaleas and rhododendrons are in full flower. A wide range of other woodland plants in genera such as *Pieris, Camellia* and *Vaccinium*, as well as numerous flowering trees, provide extra seasonal interest. All greatly appreciate the shelter provided by the canopy of oak trees.

At the top of the steps, immediately to the right is a plant of the climbing *Hydrangea petiolaris*, growing up a young oak, much as this species might do in its natural habitat. Bearing left along the path parallel to the track, to the left is a plant of the handsome large-leafed Can-

Azaleas and flowering cherries brighten the Woodland Garden in mid May

Wrought iron gates lead into the Stone Garden from the lane

ary Island holly, *Ilex platyphylla*. Effective ground cover is provided throughout this area by low shrubs such as *Gaultheria* and *Cornus canadensis*, and the attractive bright green foliage of the herbaceous *Epimedium perralderianum.* A number of flowering cherries are planted in this area, including *Prunus incisa,* grown from a sucker from an original introduction by Collingwood Ingram, renowned for his work to popularise cherries.

After making a sharp right turn at the end of the path an interesting tender pine from Mexico can be seen, *Pinus montezumae*, with long glaucous needles, planted in 1962. Nearby, plants of *Eucryphia* 'Nymansay' of the same vintage give a fine display of white flowers in mid-late summer. The area above this path was cleared and planted recently with a mixture of camellias and rhododen-

The Stone Garden, looking due north. The low hummocks of *Acer palmatum* 'Dissectum Atropurpureum' contrast with the conical *Picea glauca albertiana* 'Conica', and the bronzy-gold of *Thuja occidentalis* 'Rheingold'

drons, extending the range of species and hybrids represented.

After following the track due south, the path leading back to the Stone Garden through the wrought iron gates is to the right. Re-entering the Stone Garden area, to the left is the Temple, with a seat alongside which a number of ferns flourish in the damp shade. On the right of the seat is a fine plant of the rare moutan tree peony, *Paeonia suffruticosa* 'Rock's Variety', which has large white flowers in late spring, each petal bearing a deep maroon blotch. A strong architectural element is given by the contrasting form of upright junipers and conical dwarf conifers such as *Picea glauca albertiana* 'Conica' and *Thuja occidentalis* 'Rheingold', with the low growing hummocks of the purple-leafed Japanese maple, *Acer palmatum* 'Dissectum Atropurpureum', on either side of the path to the right. *Taxus baccata* 'Standishii' to the left of these is another fine year-round feature, with its erect habit and golden foliage.

Towards the Main Drive

To reach the Main Drive, take the grass path immediately due west of the Stone Garden, bordered by a high hedge of *Chamaecyparis pisifera* 'Squarrosa' to the left. Several clones of *Mahonia* x *media* on the right show the variation in this valuable late autumn flowering hybrid. A fine spring-flowering *Berberis valdiviana,* combines glossy evergreen foliage and saffron coloured flowers in early spring.

In the centre of the grass area leading towards the Main Drive is a tree of *Pyrus calleryana* 'Chanticleer', of upright habit, and early flowering. To the left numerous rhododendrons grow in the border on the left hand side of the drive, shaded by a fine flowering cherry, *Prunus* 'Taoyama Zakura', planted in 1961. Herbaceous plants in this bed include the rare *Lobelia laxiflora* var. *angustifolia,* with narrow tubular red and yellow flowers borne over a long season, and *Phlomis russelliana*, a yellow flowered herbaceous member of a genus usually represented in gardens by low shrubs. Further along, shaded by *Acer sieboldianum,* grows a good specimen of *Rhododendron yakushimanum*, a neat, compact bush which covers itself in spring with pink-white flowers. Effective ground-cover along the roadside is provided by the dwarf shrub *Pachysandra terminalis.*

Tennis Court and Croquet Lawn

Turning left, the steps leading up to the Old Tennis Court area are flanked with *Stephanandra incisa*, and the white rugosa rose 'Blanc Double de Coubert'. The old tennis court base was broken up in 1979, and dwarf conifers planted in low raised beds give a year round display. Amongst the unusual and rare species of conifer here are the Tasmanian *Athrotaxis cupressoides,* growing alongside the curious yew *Taxus baccata* 'Amersfoot'. A number of *Ozothamnus* (now *Helichrysum*) species from Tasmania are featured here. The most attractive is *H. ledifolius*, whose dense habit is very reminiscent of a dwarf cypress, with gold-tipped growths. Beneath it *Gunnera prorepens* from New Zealand is a pygmy of its race. A large number of dwarf cultivars of fir, spruce, pine and cypress can be seen and compared for habit and growth rate in this area.

In the border along the western flank of the Tennis Court shrub roses

A view across the Croquet Lawn in spring, with *Corylopsis* species to the right, and the white of *Magnolia kobus* to the rear

Autumn view across the Old Tennis Court, looking due north

and the attractive cupped white flowers of a *Hoheria* seedling from *H.* 'Glory of Almwch' give an attractive summer display, underplanted with a variety of hostas. Leaving the Old Tennis Court by the path in the top (south-east) corner, the Croquet Lawn is straight ahead.

The Croquet Lawn

Immediately to the right of the steps leading up to the Croquet Lawn is a planting of dwarf rhododendrons on a peat block terrace which contains the fine pink *Rhododendron trichostomum* var. *ledoides* 'Collingwood Ingram' FCC/RHS, strongly reminiscent of a daphne in its small heads of tubular pink flowers. To the left across the path the small Chilean tree *Azara microphylla* is a delicate evergreen shrub with vanilla-scented flowers in late winter. The path beyond between the Croquet Lawn and Tennis Court is bordered principally with roses and viburnums, and shaded by a large oak. At its end grows *Eucalyptus glaucescens*, attractive both for its bark and its distinctive sickle-shaped blue leaves.

The path which leads around the Croquet Lawn has a large plant of a fine evergreen New Zealand shrub, *Hoheria sexstylosa,* growing on the left. This bears numerous sprays of white flowers in midsummer. In the north-east corner of the Croquet Lawn area is a group of *Corylopsis* species. These early spring-flowering shrubs bear yellow flowers in hanging racemes, and are related to *Hamamelis*. A mixture of roses and cotoneasters covers much of the bank to the north, and at the southern end several plants of the Chilean fire bush, *Embothrium coccineum,* bear vivid orange-scarlet flowers in late spring and early summer.

The Arboretum

Following the path down towards the old Tennis Court, the entrance to the Arboretum is to the left, flanked by two examples of the fastigiate Dawyck beech, *Fagus sylvatica* 'Fastigiata', with the variegated cherry laurel *Prunus laurocerasus* 'Variegata' beneath. Aboretum plantings extend along to the stream which marks the previous southern boundary of the garden. The triangular field beyond is part of the area to be developed, although it is not expected that that will take place until the mid 1990s.

The Arboretum itself is a relatively new area of the garden, where planting began in 1975/76. The fine mature walnut tree *(Juglans regia)* which dominates the area is the point from which various rides radiate. Many interesting trees are planted here, in a wide range of genera, frequently grown from wild-source seed. The genera well represented here include *Quercus* (oaks), *Sorbus, Nothofagus* (southern beech), *Carya* (hickory), *Zelkova, Pterocarya* (wingnut), maples, birches, and a rich assortment of conifers. Plantings in the Arboretum are deliberately close, with a view to thinning-out as the trees grow, to leave a lower number of mature specimens.

The Arboretum, looking due north towards the Croquet Lawn

Immediately to the left of the Arboretum entrance a planting of small trees and shrubs provides interest and colour as the larger trees between them mature. Silver and yellow predominate, the former from *Pyrus salicifolia* 'Pendula', *P. nivalis,* and *Elaeagnus angustifolia*, whilst *Acer japonicum* 'Aureum', *Lonicera nitida* 'Baggesen's Gold' and *Pinus sylvestris* 'Aureus' are yellow as their names suggest, the latter being especially effective in winter.

A number of larger growing shrub roses also grow in this area, with several cultivars of *Rosa moyesii,* bearing single flowers from deep pink to red, and attractive flagon-shaped hips in autumn. *Rosa* 'Cerise Bouquet' is a *moyesii* hybrid, with stems up to 4 metres long (13 feet), bearing large deep cerise flowers in summer. Across the open area at the centre of the Arboretum, in the south-west corner, lies the underpass which carries the pathway back to the Visitors Centre.

Conclusion

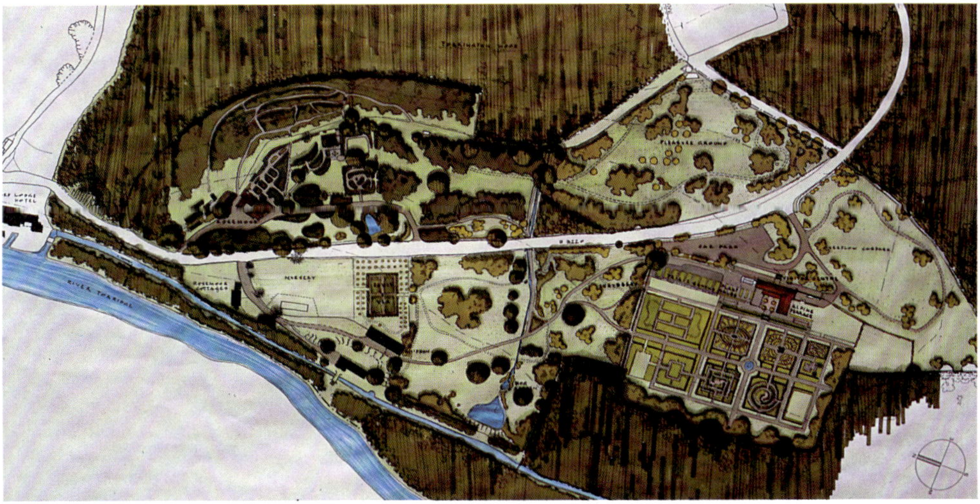

The Masterplan for Rosemoor, showing the full range of features planned for the first ten years of development

The initial development of Rosemoor as a truly national garden will take ten years. During that time the major features already described will take shape, together with others as yet only in the initial planning stage. However, many years will pass before the garden will be truly mature. Therein lies the distinctive appeal and excitement of Rosemoor, in that, uniquely, visitors and members of the Royal Horticultural Society will be able to witness this process taking place, as a national garden rises from the fields of the Rosemoor estate.

But that is by no means the whole story, for alongside the development of the garden at Rosemoor, the Society is also creating a Regional Centre for the RHS, to serve the West Country. Many activities of interest to gardeners and garden lovers already take place, centred upon Rosemoor, Cannington College in Bridgwater, Somerset, and Probus Demonstration Garden near Truro. Over the last two years Society members have been able to attend garden walks, demonstrations, workshops, lectures and short residential courses, all of which have proved extremely popular. Advice on garden problems is also available from Rosemoor, and specialist advisory staff at Wisley.

Already, Rosemoor has so much to offer the visitor, with the combination of Lady Anne's Garden and the new garden area close to the Visitors Centre, with its fine facilities. As each phase of development is completed there will be yet more to see, alongside the fascination of noting how the various parts of the garden mature. These considerations make Rosemoor very much a garden to visit again and again, and there is no better way to keep in touch with developments at Rosemoor, than by becoming a member of the RHS.

Membership of the Society carries numerous benefits. Members may visit the Society's gardens at Rosemoor and Wisley in Surrey as often as they wish, with a friend. Other gardens which offer free entry to RHS members include the Northern Horticultural Society's garden at Harlow Carr in Harrogate, Ness Gardens in the Wirral, and the Society's West Midlands Regional Centre at Pershore College in Worcestershire.

RHS members may also attend free of charge the regular Flower Shows held at Vincent Square in London, and enjoy special arrangements for attending the Chelsea Flower Show. Members also receive free of charge the excellent monthly full colour journal, The Garden.

Details of membership are available at the Entrance Kiosk, or from The Director, RHS Garden, Rosemoor, Torrington, Devon, EX38 7EG.

Written and designed by C. Bailes.
Photographs:
C. Bailes: pp. 7, 8, 10, 11, 13, 16, 17, 23, 25, 26, 27, 28, 29, 30.
E. Banks Associates: 31.
A. Lawson: 4, 19, 21, back cover.
C. J. Rougier: 15.
S. Yeo: 6.
Produced by The Reading Press Limited. Tel: (0752) 896422.

ISBN 0-906603-78-1

The Royal Horticultural Society's Garden, Rosemoor, Torrington, Devon, EX38 7EG.
Telephone 0805 24067.